CARLOS ENCINA COMMENTZ

WHEN AND HOW
TO HAVE RECOURSE TO THE
APOSTOLIC PENITENTIARY

Foreword by

FORTUNATO Card. BALDELLI

LIBRERIA
EDITRICE
VATICANA

Reprint 2020

© Copyright 2013 - Libreria Editrice Vaticana
00120 Città del Vaticano
Tel. +39 06. 698. 45780 - Fax +39 06. 698. 84716
www.libreriaeditricevaticana.com
www.vatican.va
Email: commerciale.lev@spc.va
ISBN 978-8-8266-0471-8

FOREWORD

It is my pleasure to present this publication entitled: *When and How to Have Recourse to the Apostolic Penitentiary*, by Msgr. Carlos Encina Commentz, an Official of that same Penitentiary.

Notwithstanding its long history, the Tribunal of the Apostolic Penitentiary is little known, even within the ecclesiastical world. This is in large part due to the very nature of its activity, which involves cases of the internal forum related to the Sacrament of Reconciliation.

Therefore, this small volume which I present today fills a void that has been noticed in a special way by those involved in the vast work of the Apostolic See. One sees then why this publication is timely.

Using simple conversational language accessible to all, the author has been able to present the nature of this Dicastery as an instrument of the mercy of God, describing the manner in which it works and resolves cases of conscience, which, because of their gravity, are reserved to the Holy See.

It must be clear that the silent and discreet work of the Apostolic Penitentiary has its purpose to help souls wounded by sin, but resolved to change their lives, so that they may receive the pardon of God, His mercy, and thus may begin a new life full of trust and hope.

It is my desire that these pages will be widely read.

FORTUNATO Card. BALDELLI †
Major Penitentiary

INTRODUCTION

Few priests and faithful today understand what the Apostolic Penitentiary is, what is its competency, or when and how correct recourse is made to it. For this reason, we are publishing a brief text, arranged in a question and answer format with a simple and easily understood style, so that the reader who is not a specialist in canon law can have a sufficient understanding of what the Apostolic Penitentiary is, as well as how it works. It is worth noting that this Dicastery is the oldest of the Roman Curia and that it carries out a work directly linked to the *salus animarum*.

Why is there so little knowledge about the Apostolic Penitentiary and its work?

It is not easy to answer this question. Most likely, it is due to a lack of understanding of what canon law is and to a great insufficiency of information on the competencies of the Roman Curia.

During the 60's and 70's canon law did not enjoy great respect, and there existed what could be called a widespread "anti-juridical" tendency. In brief, that current of thought viewed canon law as something contrary to the essence of the Church. Canon law was considered to be something against "charity" and as something "un-pastoral". The Gospel and the "Law of love" would be enough for the Church, because the law, according to the "anti-juridical" mode of thought, was something proper to secular society and incoherent with its way of conceiving the nature of the Church.

Before such contempt for and even rejection of canon law, the correct attitude is to try to understand its nature. Canon law is not merely a collection of positive norms of the Church. It is much more than this. The most adequate definition of canon law is: "that which is just in the Church." In other words, canon law is concerned with that which is expected of a member of the faithful and that which should be recognized, returned and given to him by others. The existence of law makes the exercise of just acts possible since justice consists precisely in giving each his due.

One can affirm with complete certainty that canon law is true law and not something "like" law or law in an analogical sense. Canon law is just as much law as is civil or procedural law. The particularities of canon law are found in its attributes and do not alter its true juridical nature.

I. THE APOSTOLIC PENITENTIARY, ITS STRUCTURE AND ITS COMPETENCY

1. What is the Apostolic Penitentiary?

The Apostolic Penitentiary is one of the Apostolic Tribunals whose competency is limited to the *internal forum*, that is, the intimate relationship between God and the individual faithful. It grants "absolutions," "dispensations," "favors," "sanations" and "commutations". The granting of indulgences has also been entrusted to the Apostolic Penitentiary.

2. What is its structure?

At the head of the Apostolic Penitentiary is the Cardinal Major Penitentiary. A Council of Prelates assists him in making decisions concerning the more complex cases. Among the prelates is the Regent, who is responsible for the organization and the smooth running of the Dicastery and who substitutes for the Cardinal Major Penitentiary in his absence. A theologian and a canonist are also members of the Council of Prelates. The Officials of this Dicastery are priests who take part in the daily meetings for the study of the cases, presided over by the Regent. They propose solutions to be then submitted to the Cardinal Major Penitentiary for his decision and signature.

3. What are the functions of the Cardinal Major Penitentiary?

All the attributes of this Dicastery are concentrated in his person. It is difficult to enumerate them considering the broad scope of cases of conscience that can be presented. It can be said that the Holy Father has entrusted to him, in the internal forum, the full exercise of the "power of the keys". In the exercise of his faculties, however, he is limited in that he cannot act without having first consulted his co-workers.

He is responsible for the appointment of Minor Penitentiaries who carry out their service in the four Papal Basilicas of Rome and the granting of faculties to them.

Another function that belongs to the Major Penitentiary is to sign the public documents, decisions and the most important correspondence of the Dicastery.

Since his important duties are related to the spiritual good of souls, he remains in authority during the vacancy of the Apostolic See. Even during the Conclave, the Tribunal has the possibility, if necessary, to send him documents that are of particular urgency.

II. COMPETENCY OF THE APOSTOLIC PENITENTIARY REGARDING DELICTS

4. What are the canonical delicts that fall under the exclusive competency of the Tribunal of the Apostolic Penitentiary in the internal forum?

There are five delicts for which the Apostolic Penitentiary has competence:

– the profanation of the Consecrated Species (cf. c. 1367 CIC);

– the direct violation of the sacramental seal of Confession (cf. c. 1388 § 1 CIC);

– the absolution of one's accomplice in a sin against the sixth commandment of the Decalogue (cf. c. 1378 § 1 CIC);

– the use of physical force against the person of the Roman Pontiff (cf. c. 1370 § 1 CIC);

– the consecration of a Bishop without a pontifical mandate (cf. c. 1382 CIC).

All of these delicts incur automatically (*latae sententiae*) the punishment of excommunication, that is, the penalty which one incurs automatically by sole the fact of having committed the delict, and for which absolution or pardon is reserved to the Apostolic See.

5. What is the delict of the profanation of the Consecrated Species?

The profanation of the Consecrated Species is a most grave delict by which one directly offends God, the Supreme Good, worthy to be loved above all things, the Creator and Lord of all that exists. It consists in the improper taking of the Eucharistic Species with sacrilegious, superstitious or obscene intentions or, more generally, in any willful and gravely disrespectful action toward the Most Holy Sacrament, whether alone or in the presence of others.

6. What is the direct violation of the sacramental seal?

This is a delict that can only be committed by a priest who has heard a confession, even if he has not given sacramental absolution. In order to violate directly the sacramental seal, it is necessary that the confessor intentionally reveal a sin he has heard during confession, as well as the identity of the penitent who confessed it. The reason this delict carries the penalty of excommunication is in order to safeguard the sacredness of the Sacrament of Penance or Reconciliation, which is the only ordinary means by which the faithful obtain pardon of their grave sins.

7. **What is meant by the absolution of one's accomplice in a sin against the Sixth Commandment of the Decalogue?**

A priest confessor who knowingly absolves his accomplice in a sin against chastity in which both have taken part commits this delict. Such an absolution, except in danger of death, is invalid and carries with it the automatic censure of excommunication. This criminal act includes all external sins committed with an accomplice in the matter of chastity, even if the sin took place before his priestly ordination. By means of this penalty, the Church protects the sacredness of the Sacrament of Penance and seeks the effective amendment of the guilty subjects. Obviously, in order to commit this delict, the confessor must be aware that he is absolving an accomplice of a sin committed by both of them together. If the confessor does not recognize the penitent, he does not commit this delict. If the accomplice does not confess a sin against chastity committed with the confessor, because it was already absolved by another confessor, the delict is not incurred.

8. **What should a confessor do when his accomplice asks for absolution?**

The confessor must, with complete frank-ness, tell the penitent that he cannot absolve the sin committed in complicity, because such an absolution would be null (cf. c. 977 CIC) and that the priest himself would also be commit-ting a most grave delict.

9. **What happens if the confessor is not aware that the penalty of excommunica-tion occurs at the moment he "absolves" an accomplice of a sin against chastity?**

In this case, ignorance does not dispense with the penalty, because it involves inexcusa-ble ignorance. All confessors who are able to exercise the ministry of confession should know the canonical norms regarding this sacrament.

10. **What does physical force against the per-son of the Roman Pontiff involve?**

It is difficult in practice for this delict to oc-cur. It involves the use of physical violence against the person of the Roman Pontiff with the intent to make an attempt on his life or to harm him.

11. What does episcopal consecration without a pontifical mandate mean?

This delict also occurs rarely. It consists in conferring the sacrament of Holy Orders upon someone, at the level of the episcopacy, without having received necessary pontifical authorization. Only a Catholic Bishop, when he carries out an Episcopal Ordination without authorization from the Roman Pontiff, can commit this delict. Such an Ordination is valid but illicit.

12. What type of canonical penalty is attached to these delicts?

The five delicts highlighted above are punished by a *latae sententiae* excommunication, which is a type of penalty incurred automatically by the very fact that certain delicts were committed. They need not be imposed by canonical process or a decree.

13. What are the effects of the penalty of excommunication?

One who is excommunicated is forbidden to:

– participate in any way as a minister in the celebration of the Eucharistic Sacrifice or in any other rite of liturgical worship;

– celebrate the sacraments or sacramentals, and to receive the sacraments;

– discharge any ecclesiastical offices or ministries or to carry out acts of pastoral governance (cf. c. 1331 § 1 CIC).

14. Why does the Catholic Church punish certain sins with canonical penalties?

The existence of a canonical penal law is a way to protect what is just in the Church. Canonical penalties also have healing, expiatory and preventive goals. For the authority of the Church, the rights of the faithful are of great importance and she seeks to protect them by various means: one of these is the imposition of canonical penalties.

15. Who can be punished by a canonical penalty?

In principle, it can be said that all the faithful of the Church who commit an external violation of a law or precept to which a penalty is attached can be punished with a canonical penalty, if that violation is gravely imputable by reason of malice or negligence (cf. c. 1321 § 1 CIC). Nevertheless, there can be certain cases that exempt or mitigate criminal responsibility. For example, those who do not have the habitual use of reason are unable to commit a canonical delict (cf. c. 1322 CIC).

16. Can a minor be punished by a canonical penalty?

In order to be punished by a canonical penalty one must have completed the sixteenth year of age (cf. c. 1323 n. 1 CIC). If one is younger than 16 years of age, he would commit a grave sin, but without incurring a canonical penalty.

17. What does it mean that an excommunication is "reserved" to the Holy See?

It means that only the Holy See can pardon that penalty. In the cases previously mentioned the competent authority in the internal forum is the Tribunal of the Apostolic Penitentiary. The fact that specific delicts are "reserved" is not due to a bureaucratic mentality, but is meant to signify that certain acts, due to their particular gravity, require special treatment. At the same time, such reservation serves the purpose of a deterrent.

18. When is it possible to absolve a penitent of an excommunication?

Excommunication, being a censure or medicinal penalty, should be absolved each time a member of the faithful is repentant of the sin he has committed. For medicinal penalties, verifying contumacy plays a fundamental role. "Contumacy" is the persistent attitude of disobedience before authority and its mandates by the one who has committed a delict. The principal purpose of medicinal penalties is that of correcting the contumacy and obtaining the conversion of the person. Medicinal penalties, therefore, cannot be imposed for a determined period of time, nor can remission be left to the arbitrary power of the superior. As soon as the contumacy ceases, remission cannot be refused since a member of the faithful has a true right to be released from it (cf. c. 1358 § 1 CIC).

19. Can an excommunicated person be absolved of his sins?

No, because the penalty of excommunication forbids the reception of the sacraments. It is necessary first to remove the excommunication and only subsequently can the penitent receive absolution from his sins.

20. Who can remit the penalty of excommunication?

Only the authority given the faculty by ecclesiastical law or one who has received proper delegation. In cases of excommunications reserved to the Apostolic See for the delicts previously discussed, the competent authority is the Apostolic Penitentiary, providing that it is a question of secret cases and that the excommunication has not been declared in the external forum.

21. When an excommunication is declared in the external forum, can the Apostolic Penitentiary remit the censure?

When an excommunication is declared in the external forum the Apostolic Penitentiary cannot intervene since it is a Tribunal of the internal forum. In order to obtain absolution one must have recourse to the competent authority.

22. Why would a canonical penalty be declared in the external forum?

In order to prevent scandal or harm to the faithful, the competent authority may have an obligation to make a *declaration*, making it known publicly that a particular subject is excommunicated. This is called the declaration of excommunication and has some juridical consequences that exacerbate the situation of the excommunicated person. For example, the remission of the penalty ceases to belong to the internal forum and must be obtained publicly in the external forum. It is one of the few cases in which a question that arises in the internal forum passes into the external forum.

23. **How should a confessor act with a penitent who is involved in a censure reserved to the Apostolic See or to the local Ordinary?**

The confessor can do three things, choosing the one that he deems most beneficial for the spiritual well-being of the penitent:

a) When the censure is reserved to the local Ordinary, the confessor can tell the penitent that – if he so desires – he can go to confession to the Diocesan Penitentiary, who has the necessary faculties to remit the censure. If the penitent does not want to go to the Diocesan

Penitentiary, the confessor can resolve the problem by choosing one of the following two options.

b) The confessor can tell the penitent that he, as confessor – in a reserved manner and without revealing names – will ask authorization permitting him to remit the censure. The penitent must return to receive remission of the censure and absolution of his sins and to receive his penance, which would be imposed by the same authority that granted the authorization to the confessor. In this case, the confessor should contact the competent authority to which the censure is reserved as soon as possible and ask authorization to remit the censure and also receive the penance that should be imposed on the penitent. For the five cases mentioned above which are reserved to the Apostolic See, the confessor should contact the Apostolic Penitentiary.

c) When it is difficult for a penitent to remain in a state of grave sin and not receive the sacraments during the time while his confessor is waiting for permission to absolve him, and if the penitent is truly sorry for the delict he has committed, the confessor can, by virtue of c. 1357 CIC, remit the penitent from the censure and absolve him from his sins, instructing him to return after several weeks at a mutually convenient time to receive the penance. In this case the confessor has the duty within 30 days to refer the case to and receive the penance from the competent authority to which the censure is reserved.

24. Is it good that the confessor use this faculty granted to him by c. 1357?

Yes, it is good that he does so. With his good counsel he can seek to lead the penitent, who would otherwise have to wait to receive the sacraments until the confessor has the faculty to absolve him, through a painful personal situation. The confessor, as a good pastor, should try to arouse in the penitent the desire to be freed from the penalty as soon as possible, to be pardoned from his sins and to receive Holy Communion.

25. How does one make recourse to the Apostolic Penitentiary?

The recourse is made through a normal and simple *letter* – typed, if possible, so as to ensure clarity – in which the confessor, leaving out the name of the penitent and any reference that could identify him, requests from the Apostolic Penitentiary the faculty to remit a censure or communicates that he has already absolved the penitent using the faculty granted by c. 1357 of the Code of Canon Law. In the letter the confessor should seek to explain objectively and concisely what took place, making reference to all the circumstances that led to the delict and that could aggravate or diminish guilt (age, state in life, etc.).

26. What information should be included in a recourse pertaining to the profanation of the Consecrated Species?

In the case of a delict for the profanation of the Consecrated Species it is necessary to include the following in the recourse:

– the approximate age of the penitent and his psychological state;

– when the delict was committed;

– how many times it was committed;

– the manner in which it was committed;

– what the motives were behind the profanation;

– whether the delict was committed by only one person or more than one;

– whether the penitent committed the delict at the instigation of a sect and, if so, whether he has broken all ties with it.

27. What information should be included in a recourse pertaining to the direct violation of the sacramental seal?

In the case of a delict for the direct violation of the sacramental seal it is necessary to include the following in the recourse:

– the approximate age of the penitent;

– when the delict was committed;

– how many times it was committed;

– the circumstances involved;

– whether the delict was committed deliberately or if it was more an act of imprudence;

– whether the person affected by the violation suffered damages;

– whether the penitent is a confessor who is normally prudent in this matter.

28. What information should be included in a recourse pertaining to the absolution of one's accomplice in a sin against the Sixth Commandment of the Decalogue?

In the case of a delict of absolution of an accomplice in a sin against the Sixth Commandment of the Decalogue it is necessary to include the following information in the recourse:

– the approximate age of the penitent;

– the approximate age of the accomplice;

– the sex of the accomplice;

– the state in life of the accomplice: single, married, religious, priest;

– how many times the accomplice was absolved;

– when was the last time that the accomplice was absolved;

– whether the penitent has ended the sinful relationship with the accomplice;

– whether the penitent is living a life worthy of his priestly calling: daily celebration of Holy Mass, fidelity to the Liturgy of the Hours, etc.

29. Why is it necessary to include all of this information in the recourse?

Including all of this information in the recourse makes possible a more just assessment of the concrete case and helps the determination of the penance that will be imposed upon the penitent and also of the duration of the concession of ministerial faculties. These elements permit the Apostolic Penitentiary to give instructions (cf. c. 1357 § 2 CIC) that can be very helpful for the penitent who is absolved of a censure.

30. Can one send a recourse by means of fax or internet?

Because a recourse deals with material usually protected by the sacramental seal, one cannot send it using electronic means like internet or fax. A letter is the best way to guarantee confidentiality in this matter, which deals with the consciences of the faithful.

31. In which languages can one write to the Apostolic Penitentiary?

One can write to this Tribunal in any existing language. In order to facilitate the work of the Officials and to receive a response in the most timely manner, it is recommended that one of the following languages be used: Italian, English, German, French, Spanish, Portuguese, Polish or Latin.

32. What heading should be placed on the envelope that is sent to the Apostolic Penitentiary?

It is sufficient to use the following address: Apostolic Penitentiary, 00120 Vatican City State.

33. Does one have to pay to make a recourse to the Apostolic Penitentiary?

Recourses to this Tribunal are *absolutely free of charge* and, in fact, not even voluntary contributions are accepted.

34. How much time does it take to receive a response from the Apostolic Penitentiary?

The Apostolic Penitentiary tries to send responses within 24 hours from the moment the recourse arrives. When the response is actually received by the confessor depends on the efficiency of the postal service of the respective country.

35. How should the confessor communicate the content of the response of the Apostolic Penitentiary to the penitent who has requested remission of a censure?

The best way to do so is within the context of a new celebration of confession. Therefore, the confessor can agree on a convenient day on which both can meet. The penitent has the right to maintain his anonymity and to not be seen, therefore this meeting with the confessor can take place in a confessional that has screens. After communicating to the penitent the content and the protocol number of the response of the Apostolic Penitentiary, the confessor should then destroy it as soon as possible. It is important that the penitent himself keep a record of the protocol number so that, if he needs to make another recourse, this Tribunal will be able to identify the case.

36. What does a rescript from the Apostolic Penitentiary fundamentally contain?

A rescript from the Apostolic Penitentiary normally contains the ratification of absolution, granted in an urgent case in virtue of what is set forth in c. 1357 CIC. If the penitent is still not absolved of the censure, the Penitentiary concedes to the confessor, by apostolic authority, the faculty to absolve of a reserved censure a well-disposed penitent.

Also, in said rescript, this Tribunal imposes a penance that the penitent is to fulfill and gives some instructions to the confessor regarding the relationship to assume with the penitent.

37. What happens if the confessor is not able to see the penitent again?

It is possible that a penitent could live elsewhere and is not able to return to the confessor who absolved him. In this case, he should give the confessor his mailing address. The confessor can then send a letter communicating a summary of the response of the Penitentiary in a way that the seal of secrecy is maintained. For example: "Grace granted. The person should pray two Rosaries every week for three months".

III. IRREGULARITIES

38. What are irregularities?

An "irregularity" is a perpetual canonical impediment, which prevents a candidate from receiving Sacred Orders or a priest from licitly exercising Orders already received, if a dispensation from the irregularity has not been obtained from the competent authority. Some irregularities presuppose delicts, but *they are not themselves canonical penalties*. As such, a person can be absolved of a delict he has committed or of all of his sins and still remain in his "irregular" condition, that is, not having obtained a dispensation. Irregularities safeguard the reverence due to sacred ministries and to the dignity of the ministers themselves. Because irregularities do not have a penal character, ignorance of them does not exempt the subject from them (cf. c. 1045 CIC).

39. Can the Apostolic Penitentiary dispense from irregularities?

When the cause of the irregularities that prevent the reception of Holy Orders and the exercise of Orders already received is not a publicly known fact, the Apostolic Penitentiary can grant dispensations from them. This Tribunal has the competency to dispense in the internal forum from irregularities reserved to the Holy See, in particular those involving one who has committed or positively cooperated in the crime of murder or the procurement of an abortion (cf. c. 1041 n. 4; 1044 § 1 n. 3 CIC). Even though it is clear that not all irregularities are reserved to the Holy See and that in many cases the diocesan Bishop has the faculty to dispense from them, the faithful are free to have recourse to the Apostolic Penitentiary.

40. How does one request a dispensation from an irregularity from the Penitentiary?

The request for dispensation from an irregularity is submitted by means of a letter written to the Apostolic Penitentiary by the confessor or the spiritual director of the one who is irregular. The request should omit the name of the person and explain clearly what brought about the state of irregularity. If the request deals with a candidate for Holy Orders, the confessor or spiritual director should include his judgment concerning the person's suitability to receive the sacrament. If it deals with a person who is already ordained, it is important to make reference to his amended way of life.

41. Why are irregularities dealt with in the "internal forum": can a dispensation be obtained outside of confession?

An act that makes one irregular could be something secret and, therefore, it is best that it be resolved in the internal forum. If a person becomes aware of his irregularity through a conversation with a priest, he can ask for a dispensation without having confessed it. In this case it is helpful to use the non-sacramental internal forum which is also protected by secrecy.

42. What happens if a person in an irregular state receives Holy Orders?

In this case, he can continue to exercise his Orders if the case is secret and he cannot have recourse to the Ordinary or the Penitentiary, and if there would be serious danger of harming his reputation. The recourse should be made as soon as possible to the competent authority by means of the confessor or the person's spiritual director (cf. c. 1048 CIC).

43. When should recourse be made to the Apostolic Penitentiary when dealing with a candidate for Orders who is affected by an irregularity?

The request for a dispensation from an irregularity for a candidate for Orders is usually sent as soon as the candidate has been approved for Sacred Orders. Such approval is a sign of the candidate's suitability, to which reference in the request should be made. As a practice, the Apostolic Penitentiary examines the requests speedily so that the confessor or spiritual director of the candidate will have the response in hand within a few days.

IV. RETROACTIVE CONVALIDATION OF MARRIAGES

44. Can the Apostolic Penitentiary retroactively convalidate an invalid marriage?

The Apostolic Penitentiary can retroactively convalidate a marriage contracted invalidly when, for just reasons, it would be best to do so in the internal forum. For example, it may not be desirable to publicize the retroactive convalidation of a marriage that is considered by all to be valid. For this to occur it must be a marriage that is truly willed and in which it can be presumed that the parties desire to continue to live together. The competent authority for granting a retroactive convalidation of a marriage is normally the diocesan Bishop but, for just reasons, recourse can be made to the Holy See (see the definition of retroactive convalidation in c. 1161 § 1 CIC).

45. Is it necessary that both parties be aware of and request the retroactive convalidation?

Not necessarily. The request for a retroactive convalidation can be made by both or by one of the parties, even without the other's knowledge. The priest who has obtained the retroactive convalidation of a marriage by means of a rescript of the Apostolic Penitentiary should insert the names of both parties on the same rescript, which will remain in the secret archives of the diocesan Curia. It is important that the person or the persons seeking a retroactive convalidation retain the protocol number of the rescript in case it would be necessary to verify the retroactive convalidation in the future. However, if the priest has received information regarding the invalidity of the marriage through confession, the rescript of the Apostolic Penitentiary should be destroyed as soon as its content is communicated and the protocol number is given to the petitioner(s).

V. MASS OBLIGATIONS

46. Does the Apostolic Penitentiary have competency in matters concerning the obligation to celebrate Holy Mass?

Having accepted a Mass intention and having received an offering for its celebration constitutes a serious obligation of justice for the priest who must either satisfy it personally or by means of another priest. If a priest has received a large number of Mass intentions and for whatever reason finds it impossible to celebrate them, he may, by means of his confessor, ask the Apostolic Penitentiary to reduce his Mass obligations.

47. Can the Apostolic Penitentiary grant reductions of Holy Mass obligations that fall to juridical persons or institutions because of legacies received?

In cases when obligations to celebrate Mass fall to juridical persons or institutions, for example a seminary or the Diocesan Curia, the Penitentiary cannot grant this type of grace. Contrary to the above case where the obligations fall to the soul of the individual priest whose good reputation must be protected, these cases deal with matters of the external forum, and recourse must be made to the Congregation for the Clergy.

48. How should a confessor proceed when a priest informs him that he has received Mass intentions but has been unable to fulfill them?

A repentant priest who finds it impossible to celebrate Masses for which he has received stipends can request, through his confessor, that a reduction be granted to him. The confessor, omitting the name of the penitent priest, should write a letter to the Apostolic Penitentiary indicating the following:

– the number of Masses that were not fulfilled;

– the approximate age of the priest;

– the reason why he did not fulfill his obligation and how he spent the money received for them;

– his state of health and the number of Masses that he can fulfill personally or with the assistance of other priests.

The Apostolic Penitentiary, after evaluating all the information contained in the recourse, will proceed with the reduction of the number of Masses that were not fulfilled by the penitent priest, imposing the obligation to celebrate or to arrange for the celebration of a small number of them, the remaining obligation being fulfilled from the "treasury of the Church"[1]. The Cardi-

---

[1] The expression "treasury of the Church" is not to be understood as the sum total of material goods that the Church possesses, but as the infinite and inexhaustible

nal Major Penitentiary informs the Holy Father in private audience of each case involving the reduction of Mass obligations.

VI. OTHER CASES

49. Is it possible to submit questions of a moral or canonical nature to the Tribunal of the Apostolic Penitentiary?

Obviously the priest or person who has a doubt of a moral or canonical nature should try to resolve it by consulting Magisterial texts of the Church or the opinion of approved authors before having recourse to the Tribunal of the Penitentiary. Considering, however, the complexity of some cases which priests encounter in the exercise of their ministry, it is possible to submit concrete questions of a moral or canoni-

---

value that the expiation and the merits of our Lord Jesus Christ have before God, as well as the immense value of the prayers and good works of the Most Blessed Virgin Mary and all the Saints (cf. CLEMENT VI, *Jubilee Bull Unigenitus Dei Filius* in Paul VI, Apost. Const. *Indulgentiarum doctrina*).

cal nature involving specific cases to the Tribunal of the Apostolic Penitentiary, without mentioning the names of the persons who may be involved. This Dicastery, after consulting its experts in the more complex cases, will send a response indicating how one should proceed in that particular situation.

VII. INDULGENCES

50. Can the Apostolic Penitentiary grant indulgences?

The Apostolic Penitentiary is the Dicastery of the Roman Curia that is competent to *grant* indulgences. A request for an indulgence is usually made by means of letter or fax, indicating the reason for the request and including the signature of the Diocesan Bishop who must approve the request. The request for an indulgence should be sent in a timely manner so that the decree can be forwarded in due time. In recent years there has been a notable increase in the number of requests for indulgences.

CONCLUSION

It is hoped that after reading these questions and responses the reader will have gained an understanding of the Apostolic Penitentiary, a body at the service of confessors and penitents. For good reason it is called "The Tribunal of Mercy," because its principal mission is to help a member of the faithful, who finds himself in a situation incompatible with his eternal salvation, to be reconciled with God and the Church. The Apostolic Penitentiary does not exercise its jurisdiction in a way that the authorities of the external forum do since the anonymity of the person is always protected. Neither is there a competition between parties defending their own interests: the Apostolic Penitentiary is not a tribunal to which a person turns to so as to punish another member of the faithful.

The existence of an internal forum in the Church is a good of inestimable value and is often little understood by one who does not know the ways of God. The internal forum is directly concerned with salvation of souls, and it is important that it exist so that a member of the faithful does not suffer damage to his good reputation and can begin anew a life in harmony with God. Furthermore, no one has a "right to know everything about everyone," and publicizing evil can have negative effects both for the specific individual and for the surrounding community.

A good shepherd, he who seeks out the lost sheep, should have great esteem for the internal forum and defend it heroically. This does not mean that one "covers up evil" but that one cooperates with the plan of God for the salvation of people. At the end of this earthly pilgrimage, each one of us will be judged by God, and His judgment will be perfect, free of all error, and in Him the divine attributes of mercy and justice will be mysteriously combined. We should not forget the words of the Lord: "I tell you, there will be more joy in heaven over one sinner who repents than over ninety-nine righteous persons who need no repentance" (*Luke* 15:7).

TABLE OF CONTENTS

www.ingramcontent.com/pod-product-compliance
Lightning Source LLC
LaVergne TN
LVHW031436170726
843492LV00010B/3035